dabble lab

10-MINUTE
FUN and EASY
PROJECTS

65 Craft Activities You Can Make in a Flash

BY CHRISTOPHER HARBO,
SARAH L. SCHUETTE, AND TAMMY ENZ
ILLUSTRATED BY LUCY MAKUC

CAPSTONE PRESS
a capstone imprint

TABLE OF CONTENTS

GOT 10 MINUTES?

When it comes to making crafts, you don't need a lot of time to have a ton of fun!

These quick and easy projects will delight you. Ask an adult to help you, grab some supplies, and then get making!

GENERAL SUPPLIES AND TOOLS

acrylic paint

aluminum foil

balloons

bottle caps

button magnets

cardboard

chopsticks

clothespins

colored pencils

construction paper

contact paper

cord

craft sticks

crayons

decoupage glue

disposable cups
electrical tape
eraser caps
erasers
glitter
glue
googly eyes
hammer and nail
hole punch
hot glue gun
magazines
markers
measuring cups
metal washers
nails
origami paper
pencils

pencil sharpener
pipe cleaners
poster board
printer paper
recycled lids, bottles,
  cans, cups
rubber bands
ruler
scissors
screwdriver
sewing needle
sewing thread
stapler
straws
string
tape
tin cans
toothpicks
utility knife
wrapping paper
yarn

TIPS

- Before starting a project, gather the supplies and tools needed.

- Ask an adult to help you with sharp or hot tools.

- When drawing, sketch lightly at first and don't be afraid to make mistakes. Simply use an eraser to remove any unwanted lines.

- Practice makes perfect when it comes to origami! The more times you fold a model, the better it will look.

- When weaving or wrapping something large in yarn, leave the yarn attached to the ball to make sure you have enough.

- If you cut the yarn too short to finish a project, tie on another piece and keep going.

- There's no right or wrong way to make these projects! Experiment and use your imagination.

- Change things up! Don't be afraid to make your projects your own.

KITTEN

If you like drawing cats, you've come to the right place. This curious kitty is as cute as a button!

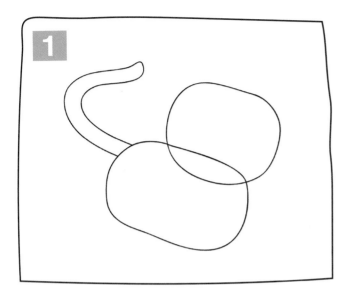

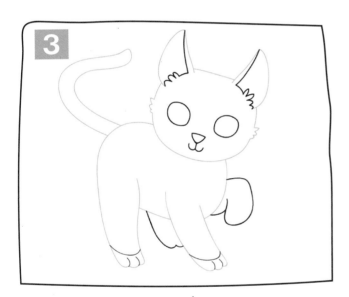

TIP Draw a collar, bow, or bell on your kitten to really make it your own.

PUPPY

If puppies are more your style, you're in luck. This playful pooch will practically leap off the page with a few simple steps.

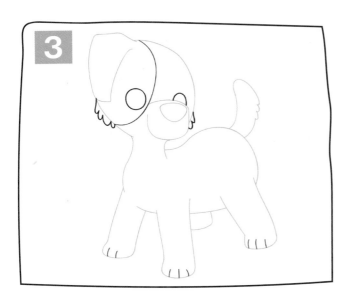

TIP Changing up your pup is simple. Just add a pattern or texture to her coat, such as spots, stripes, or curly hair!

PONY

What gets a pony prancing? A tasty treat
of course! Draw this happy horse as it
munches on a sweet, juicy apple!

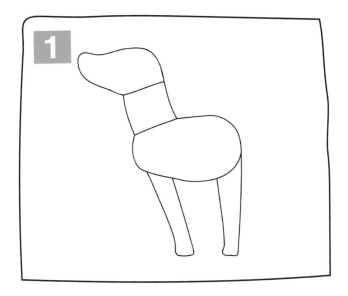

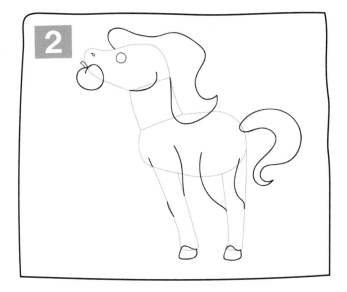

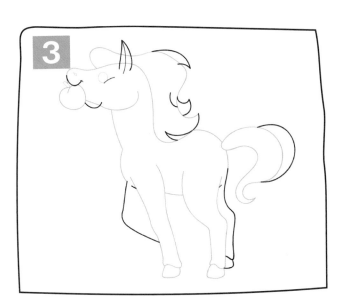

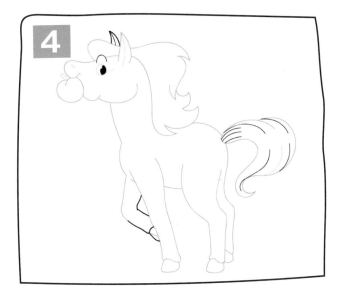

TIP Apples aren't the only things ponies like to snack on. Try switching out the apple with a carrot or a stalk of celery.

ANGELFISH

Glub, glub, glub. Go on an underwater adventure
by learning to draw this amazing angelfish!

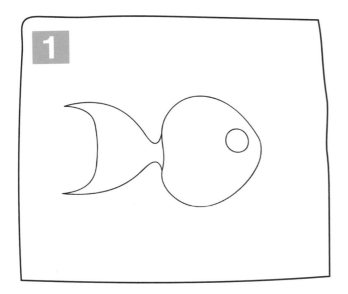

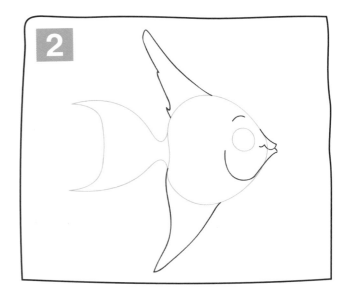

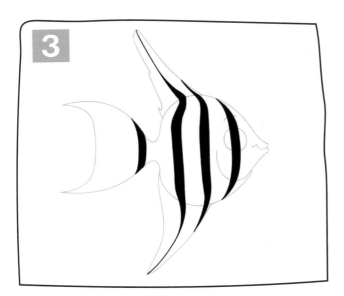

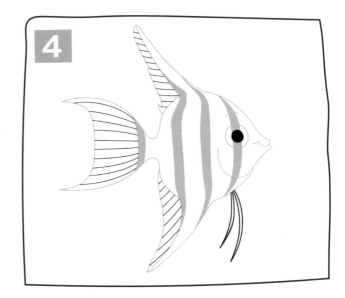

TIP Draw more types of fish by changing the size and shape of the angelfish's body. There's no limit to the kinds of fish you can create!

SPIDER

Don't let this little guy scare you. He may
have eight hairy legs, but this super-simple
spider is a cinch to draw.

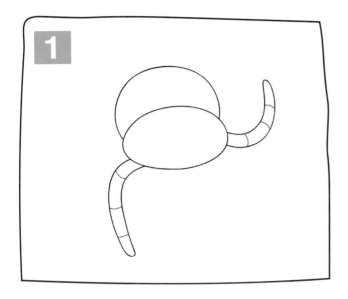

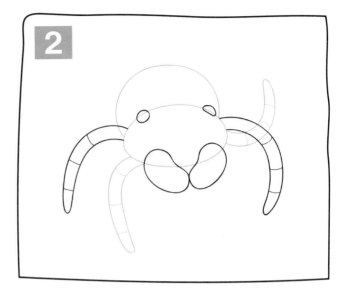

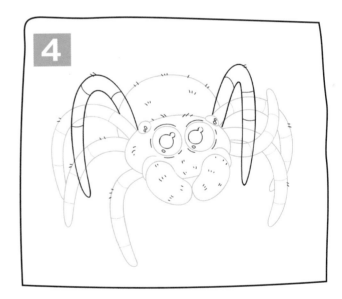

TIP Turn your tiny spider into a mutant monster. Just add mini houses, trees, and people around his legs to make him a towering titan!

ROBOT

One day, robots may help you do everything—
even clean your room! Until that happens, test
your art skills on this friendly bot.

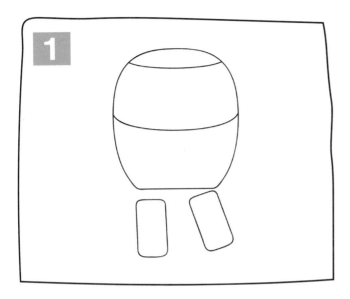

TIP Add a background that tells a story. Computer panels could show that your robot is on board a spacecraft. A junkyard could mean he's been tossed in the trash!

SPACE ALIEN

Greetings from the cosmos! Draw this friendly space alien as he waves hello from a passing asteroid.

TIP Draw one large alien and two smaller space aliens on either side of him. You'll create a whole space alien family!

MONSTER

Imagine you are hiking in the mountains without a camera when you cross paths with this monster. What are you going to do? Draw it, of course!

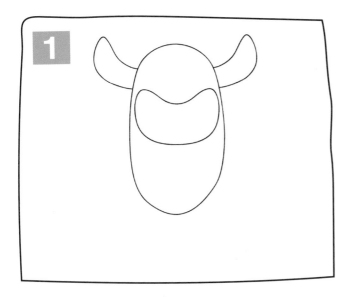

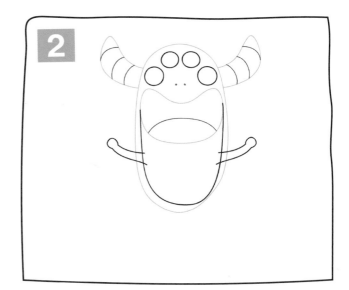

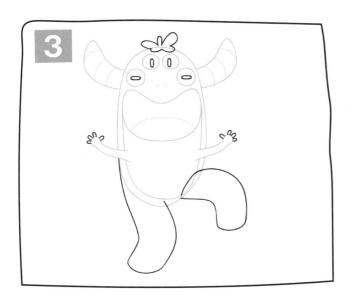

TIP Use your imagination to modify your monster! Add arms, legs, or even more heads to make it truly one of a kind.

RACE CAR

VROOM! VROOM! VROOM! Now's your chance to draw the race car of your dreams. Just sharpen your pencils and you'll be off to the races!

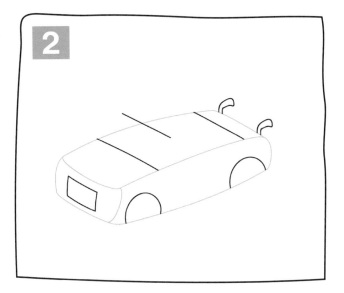

TIP Make your race car look like it is roaring down the track. Just add a few motion lines off the back of the car to give some ZOOM to its vroom!

JET

When it comes to drawing, it never hurts to set
your sights high. Do just that with a sleek jet
that glides through the clouds.

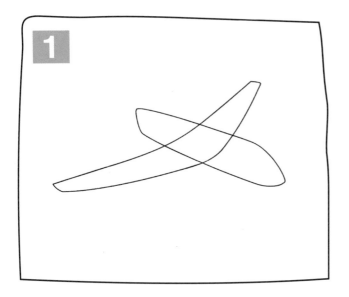

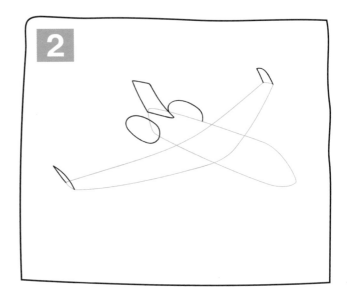

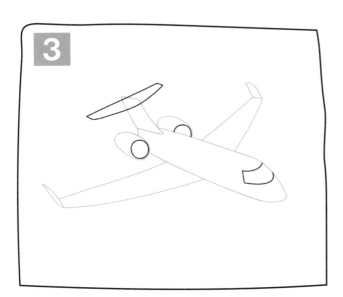

TIP Where in the world is your jet?
Add a background, such as mountains or
a famous landmark, to help tell a story.

SPACESHIP

3, 2, 1, blast off! Imagine yourself soaring through the solar system as you draw this simple spaceship.

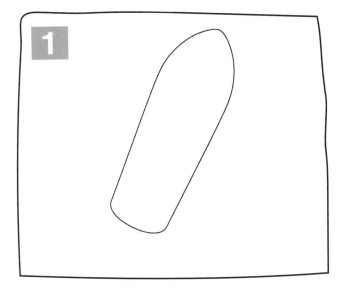

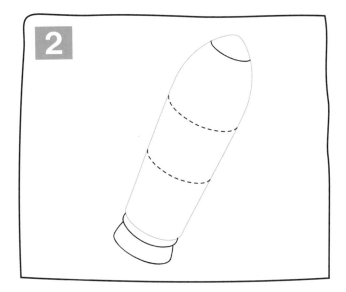

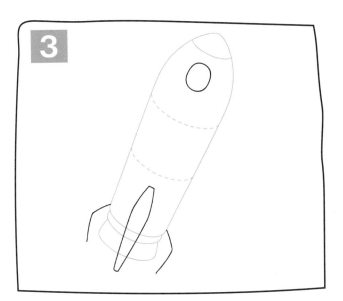

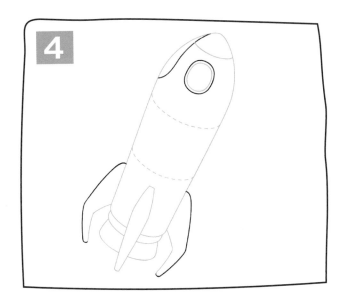

TIP Every spacecraft needs a pilot. Draw an astronaut or alien waving out the window. You decide!

SUNFLOWER

Need a quick way to brighten your day? Draw this
stunning sunflower in just 10 minutes or less!

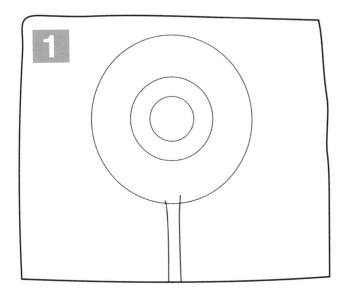

TIP Change the shape of the petals to create daisies, pansies, and other kinds of flowers.

CASTLE

Hear ye, hear ye! Test your skills by drawing a royal palace that would be perfect for any king or queen.

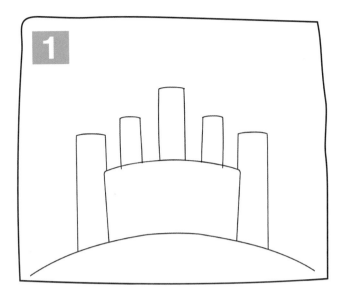

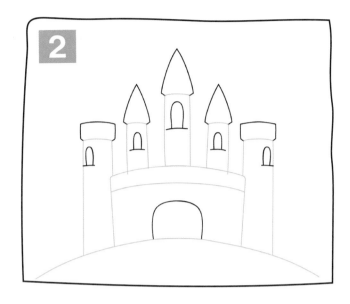

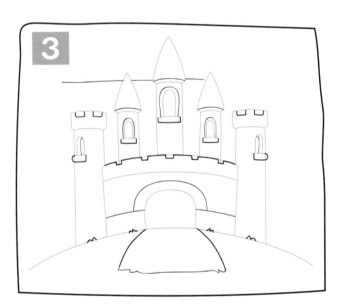

TIP Try adding extra details to your castle. Decorate the pointed towers with flags. Or add walls on the left and right to turn your castle into a fortress!

MARSHMALLOW TARGET SHOOT

What can you do with marshmallows, a balloon, and a few common supplies? Whip up this cool game that can be played anywhere.

What You Need:

disposable cup
utility knife
balloon
scissors
1 sheet of construction paper
tape
marshmallows

What You Do:

1 Ask an adult to cut out the bottom of the cup with the utility knife.

2 Tie the open end of the balloon in a knot. Snip off the other end of the balloon with the scissors.

3 Stretch the snipped end of the balloon over the cup's bottom. Wrap the balloon around the sides of the cup.

4 Cut a piece of construction paper in half lengthwise. Tape the two halves end-to-end to make a long strip.

5 Loop the strip of construction paper into a circle and tape it together to make a hoop.

6 Set the hoop on the floor. Stand about five paces away. Place a marshmallow in the cup and pull back the balloon's knot. Release the knot to launch the marshmallow into the hoop.

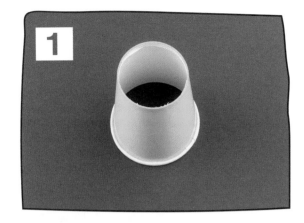

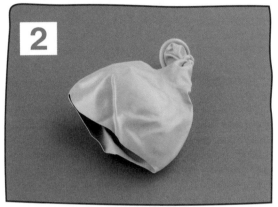

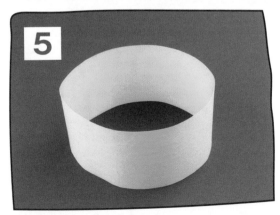

TIP Make several hoops of different sizes. Give each a point value and then test your skill at shooting into the hoops.

39

CANDY LAUNCHER

Clothespins can do more than just hang your laundry. Harness their power to make a launcher that can shoot candy across the room!

What You Need:

clothespin
small block
of wood
hot glue gun
craft stick

utility knife
ruler
bottle cap
candy

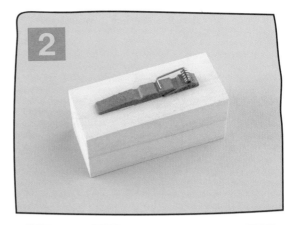

What You Do:

1 Take a clothespin apart. Then turn the spring around and place it backward on one half of the clothespin.

2 Center the flat side of the clothespin on the block of wood. Hot glue the clothespin in place.

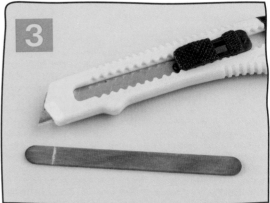

3 Ask an adult to use the utility knife to carve a notch about 0.5 inch (1 cm) from the end of the craft stick.

4 Slide the craft stick into place so the notch is under the spring.

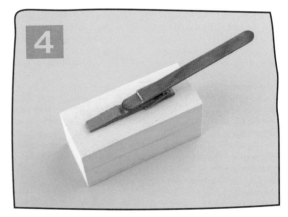

5 Hot glue the bottle cap to the other end of the craft stick. Leave the last 0.25 inch (0.6 cm) of the stick showing so you can push on it.

6 Place a small candy in the cap. Push the stick down as far as possible. Release the stick to send the candy flying.

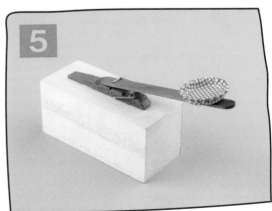

TIP Use your launcher to fling other small objects, such as beads, coins, or tiny toys.

LOOP HOOPS

How good is your hand-eye coordination? Test it out with a classic game you can build yourself.

What You Need:

marker
mini disposable cup
orange table tennis ball
nail
hot glue gun
18-inch- (46-cm-) long piece
   of string
chopstick

What You Do:

1 Draw lines on the table tennis ball and the cup to make them look like a basketball and a hoop.

2 Punch a hole in the bottom of the cup with the nail.

3 Glue the ball to one end of the string. Thread the other end of the string through the bottom of the cup. Tie a large knot on the end of the string.

4 Push the tip of the chopstick into the bottom of the cup. Glue it in place.

5 Holding the chopstick, swing the ball up and try to catch it in the cup.

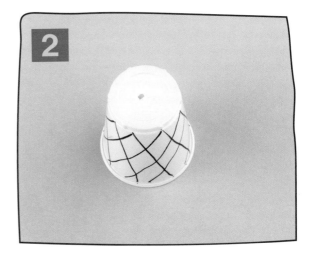

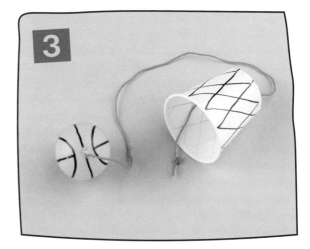

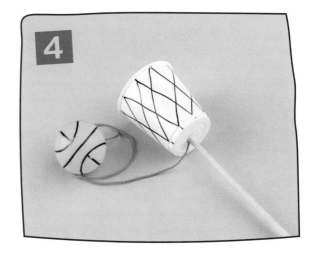

TIP To increase the challenge, try attaching a longer string to the ball and cup.

43

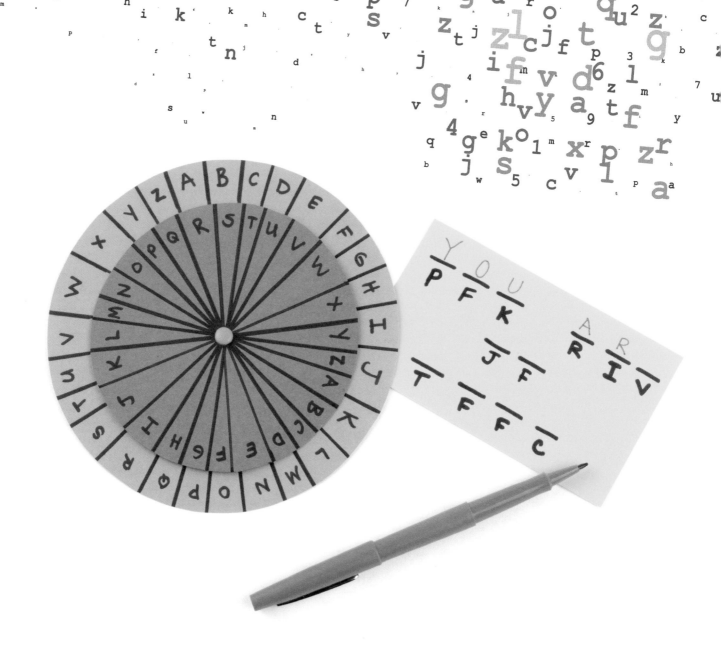

CIPHER WHEEL

Protect your secret notes from prying eyes.
Build a cipher wheel to send and solve coded
messages between friends.

What You Need:

construction paper
CD
cereal bowl
marker
scissors
ruler
brass fastener
pencil and paper

What You Do:

1 Place the CD and the cereal bowl, face down, on the construction paper. Trace around both objects and cut out the circles.

2 Mark the center of the small circle. Place a ruler on this mark and draw a line to divide the circle in half.

3 Make 12 equally spaced marks on each half of the circle. Use the ruler and marker to connect these marks by drawing lines through the center of the circle. Label each section from "A" through "Z."

4 Stack the small circle on the large circle. Connect them in the center with a brass fastener.

5 Extend the lines of the small circle onto the large circle. Label these sections "A" through "Z" too.

6 Write a message on a piece of paper. Spin the circles so like letters don't line up. Code the message by replacing each letter used from the large circle with the letter it's next to on the small circle.

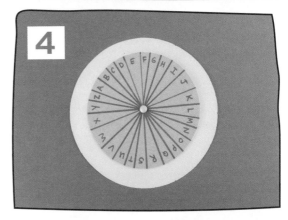

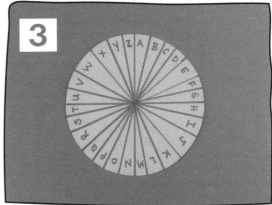

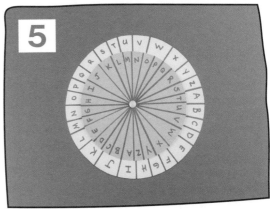

TIP Help friends decode your messages by telling them which letter on the small circle lines up with the A on the large circle.

CELL PHONE AMP

Don't let a small cell phone speaker spoil your dance tunes. Make this handy amp to pump up the volume!

What You Need:

marker
paper towel tube
2 sheets of construction paper
scissors
2 disposable cups
tape
utility knife

What You Do:

1 Trace around one end of the tube on a piece of construction paper. Cut out the circle and tape it to the side of a cup. Make sure the circle sits about 0.5 inch (1 cm) from the bottom of the cup.

2 Ask an adult to cut around the circle with a utility knife. Remove the tape.

3 Repeat steps 1 and 2 with the other cup.

4 Roll the other sheet of construction paper around the tube and tape it in place. Stick the ends of the tube into the holes in the cups.

5 Ask an adult to cut a slit on the top of the paper towel tube with a utility knife. Make the slit just large enough to fit a cell phone.

6 Slide your phone into the slit and play some music.

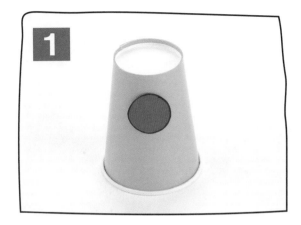

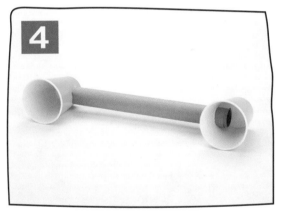

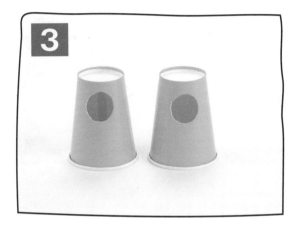

MINI FLICK FLASHLIGHT

This mini flashlight is powerful, easy to make, and holds a secret. Just a flick of the wrist will turn it on.

What You Need:

small tin box
hammer and nail
mini LED bulb
electrical tape
CR2032 button battery
mini tilt switch
wire clip
hot glue gun

What You Do:

1 Use the hammer and nail to punch a hole in one end of the box. Make the hole large enough to fit the tip of the LED bulb.

2 Tape the long leg of the LED to the positive (+) side of the battery.

3 Tape one of the tilt switch legs to the negative (-) side of the battery.

4 Clip the short leg of the LED to the remaining leg on the tilt switch. Tilt the circuit back and forth to see the LED light up.

5 Place the circuit in the box so the LED shines out of the hole. Glue the battery to the bottom of the box.

6 Close the box. Flick the box up or down when you need a flashlight.

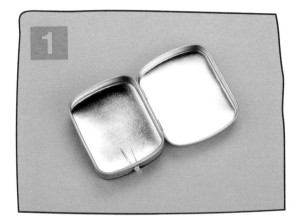

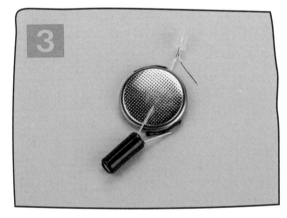

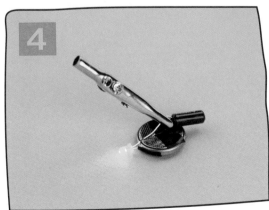

TIP Tilt switches and LEDs can be found at most hobby stores and electronics shops.

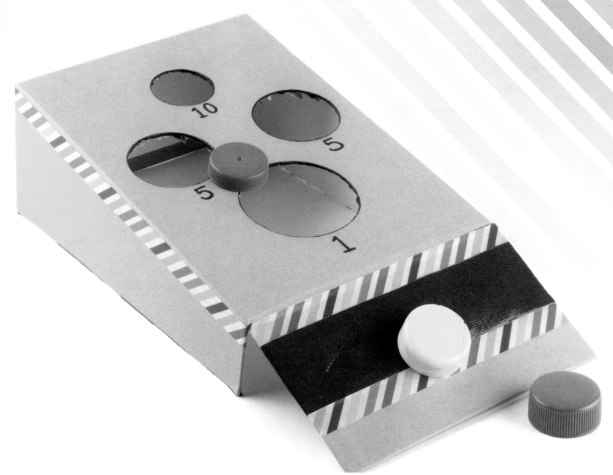

BULL'S-EYE SHOOTER

No festival or fair is complete without
a Skee-Ball game. Now you can whip up
this mini version to play on the go.

What You Need:

shoebox
ruler
marker
scissors
small bowl
small cup
milk cap
water bottle cap

What You Do:

1 Open the flap on one end of the box.

2 Use the marker and ruler to draw a diagonal line from the middle of the open end to the corner of the closed end. Cut along this line.

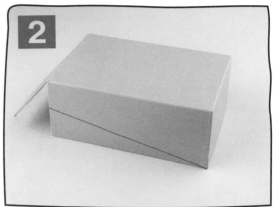

3 Repeat step 2 on the other side of the box. Set the box facedown so it looks like a ramp.

4 Place the bowl, cup, milk cap, and water bottle cap on the ramp. Trace around each object, then remove and cut out the circles.

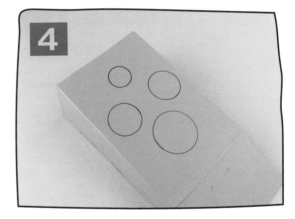

5 Label all of the circles with points. Give the large circles small point values and the small circles large point values.

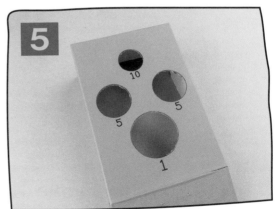

6 Place the water bottle cap at the bottom of the ramp. Flick it with your finger to try to make it go into an opening. Add up your score after five tries.

TIP Flick the cap from different angles to try to hit different holes.

51

BALLOON HOVER GAME

Here's a game that will leave you breathless.
See how long you can keep a balloon hovering
with lung power!

What You Need:

disposable cup
ruler
pencil
scissors

bendable straw
hot glue gun
balloon

What You Do:

1 Measure 1.5 inches (4 cm) from the bottom of the disposable cup. Draw a line around the cup at this mark.

2 Cut along the line. Discard the top of the cup.

3 Poke a small hole in the bottom of the cup with the scissors.

4 Bend the straw and stick the short end into the hole. Glue around the straw inside the cup to hold it in place.

5 Blow up the balloon and tie it closed.

6 Set the balloon on the cup. Blow into the straw to make the balloon hover.

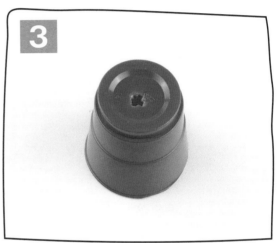

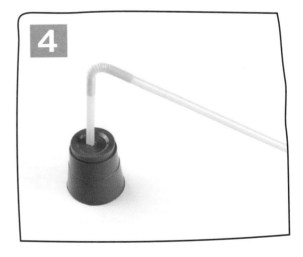

TIP Make a pair of hover balloons. Then challenge a friend to see who can keep a balloon in the air longer.

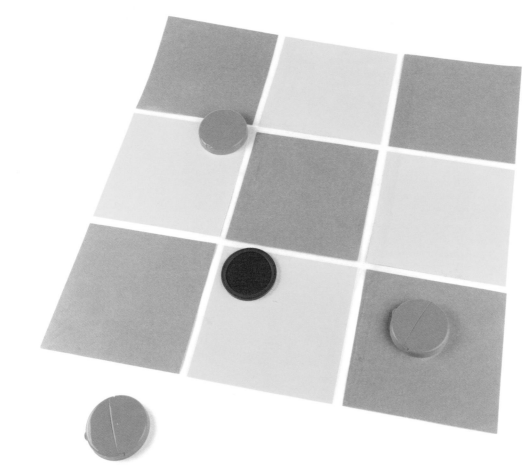

TIC-TAC-TOSS MAT

Give a game of tic-tac-toe a clever twist.
Make a giant game board and fling
plastic lids as X's and O's.

What You Need:

ruler
clear contact paper
9 10-inch (25-cm) squares of
    poster board (two colors)
scissors
10 plastic lids (two colors)

What You Do:

1 Cut one 31-inch- (79-cm-) long strip of contact paper. Lay it on a flat surface sticky side up.

2 Place three poster board squares on the contact paper, alternating the colors. Leave a 0.5-inch (1-cm) gap between them.

3 Repeat steps 1 and 2 with two more strips of contact paper and the remaining poster board to create a checkerboard pattern.

4 Cover the top of the squares with three more 31-inch- (79-cm-) long strips of contact paper. Trim off any extra edges.

5 Place the mat on the floor and challenge a friend to a game of tic-tac-toe. Stand 10 steps away from the mat and take turns flinging the plastic lids. The first person to connect three squares in a row wins!

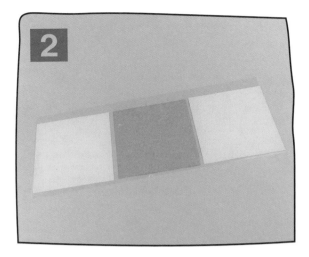

GIANT BUBBLE BLOWER

No summer is complete without a little bubble blowing. Take your bubbles to the next level with this nifty gadget.

What You Need:

plastic bottle
utility knife
1/8 cup (30 mL) dish soap
1/8 cup (30 mL) light corn syrup
1 teaspoon (5 mL) glycerin
1/4 cup (60 mL) hot water
bowl
spoon

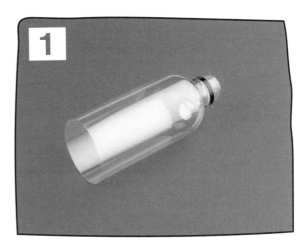

What You Do:

1 Ask an adult to cut off the bottom half of the bottle with a utility knife. Recycle the bottom of the bottle. Set the top of the bottle aside.

2 Mix the soap, syrup, glycerin, and water in the bowl. Stir slowly with the spoon.

3 Dip the cut edge of the bottle top in the mixture.

4 Blow through the bottle's spout to make giant bubbles.

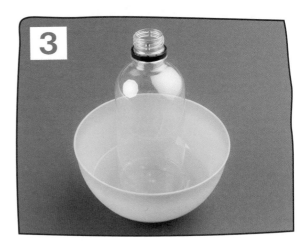

TIP Use this bubble blower outdoors on a breezy day to see the bubbles float up and away.

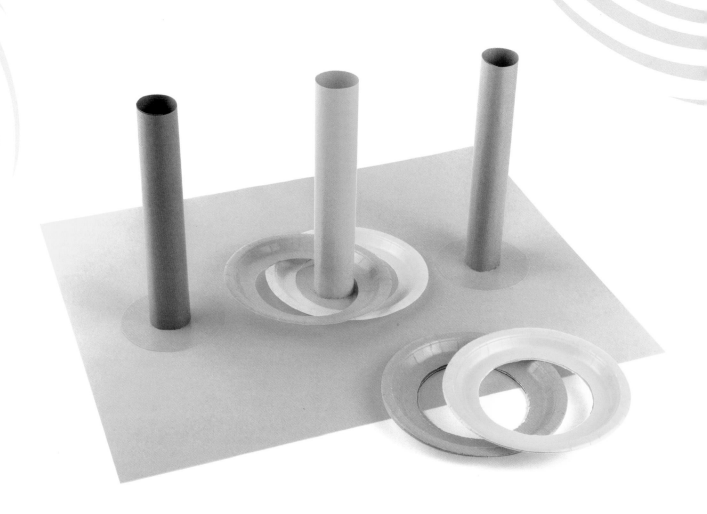

RING FLING

Ring toss is a popular party game.
Make your own version in minutes with
just a few simple supplies.

What You Need:

3 sheets of construction paper, each a different color

tape

hot glue gun

1 sheet of poster board

10 paper plates (two colors)

scissors

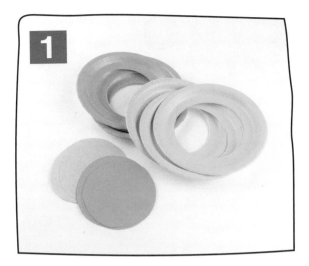

What You Do:

1 Cut the center out of each paper plate. These are your rings.

2 Roll each sheet of paper into a tube about 2 inches (5 cm) wide. Tape the edges of each tube to hold it in place.

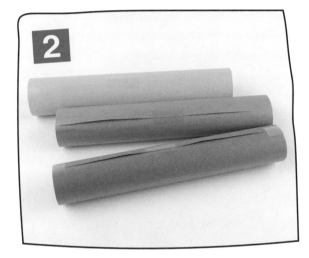

3 Glue the tubes to the circles cut from the paper plates in step 1.

4 Glue the circles and tubes to the poster board. Place them about 12 inches (30 cm) apart.

5 Place the game board on the floor and take 10 steps back.

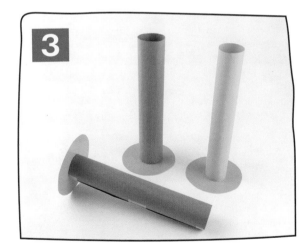

6 Give a friend five rings of the same color. Take turns tossing them at the tubes.

TIP Assign points to each tube. For instance, one point for the closest tube, two points for the middle tube, and three points for the farthest tube.

KNOCK HOCKEY

Clear off a table or desk! With just a couple of goals and some chopsticks, you'll have your very own hockey rink.

What You Need:

12 bendable straws
hot glue gun
2 water bottles
milk cap
2 chopsticks

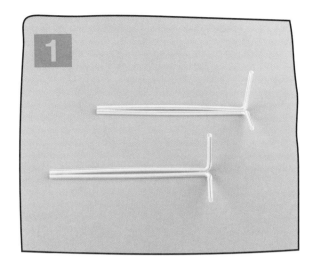

What You Do:

1 Bend two straws into 90-degree angles. Glue their long sides together to make a goalpost. Repeat this step with a second pair of straws.

2 Slide a straw between the goalposts to make a crossbar. The crossbar should sit about 5 inches (13 cm) above the bent legs of the goalposts.

3 Adjust the legs of the goalposts so the goal stands by itself.

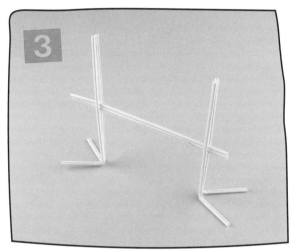

4 Repeat steps 1 through 3 to make another goal.

5 Place the goals on opposite ends of a table. Stand water bottle goalies 2 inches (5 cm) in front of each goal.

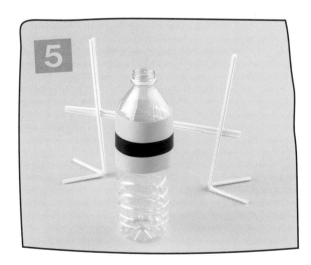

6 Set the milk cap "puck" in the center of the table. Take turns flicking the puck with a chopstick to try to shoot it through the goalposts.

TIP Make up your own rules! What happens if you hit the puck off the table without going through the goal? Maybe your opponent gets two shots in a row from the middle of the table.

MINI BOWLING ALLEY

Bowling is a game of skill and determination.
See how your game measures up with this
easy-to-make mini alley.

What You Need:

- 24-inch- (61-cm-) long board
- 2 1-inch- (2.5-cm-) long drywall screws
- screwdriver
- milk cap
- hammer and nail
- 6-inch- (15-cm-) long rubber band
- table tennis ball
- markers
- 6 corks

What You Do:

1 Lay the board flat. Screw the drywall screws into the board about 4 inches (10 cm) from one end. Place each screw about 0.25 inch (0.6 cm) from each side of the board. Screw them in only halfway.

2 Use the hammer and nail to make two holes in the milk cap. Make the holes about 0.5 inch (1 cm) apart. Thread the rubber band through the holes on the underside of the cap.

3 Adjust the loops so they extend equally from the top of the cap. Place each loop over a screw.

4 Use markers to decorate the table tennis ball with "finger holes" and the board with bowling lane arrows.

5 Place the corks on the other end of the board in a triangle formation.

6 Set the ball between the screws. Draw back the cap and let it go to launch the ball at the pins.

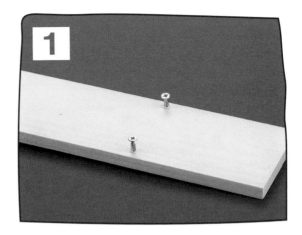

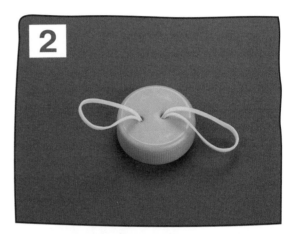

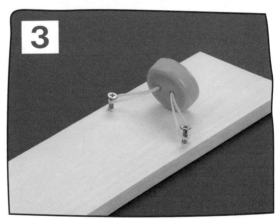

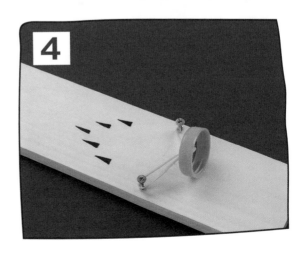

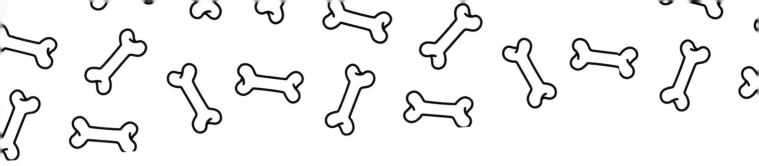

HAPPY HOUND

Folding this paper pup is easier than
walking a dog! With just four simple steps,
you'll have a floppy-eared pooch.

What You Need:

square origami paper
glue, markers, googly eyes,
and pom-pom (optional)

1

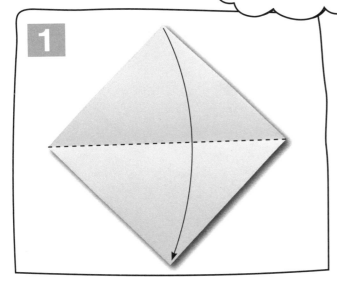

Fold the top point to the bottom point.

2

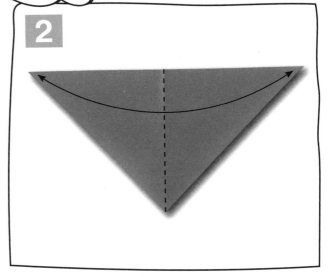

Fold the left point to the right point
and unfold.

3

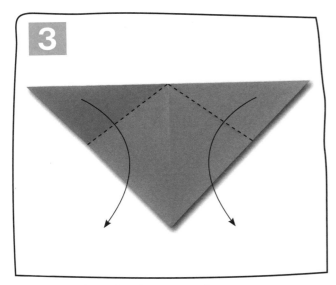

Fold the left and right points down.

4

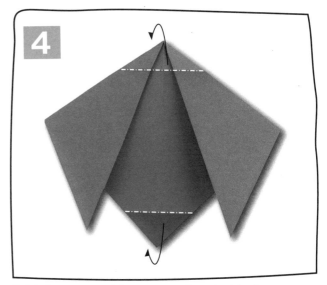

Fold the top and bottom points behind
the model.

TIP Add personality to your pup. Use markers, googly
eyes, and a pom-pom to give it an adorable face.

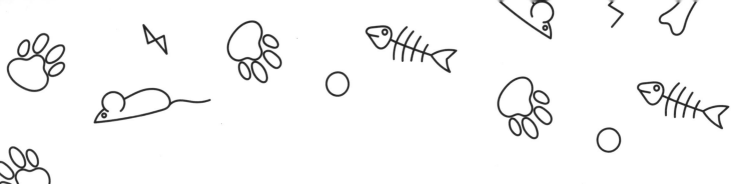

CLEVER CAT

You can tell a cat is curious when its ears perk up. This clever model captures that look with purr-fectly pointy ears!

What You Need:

square origami paper
glue and button magnet
(optional)

1

Fold the bottom point to the top point.

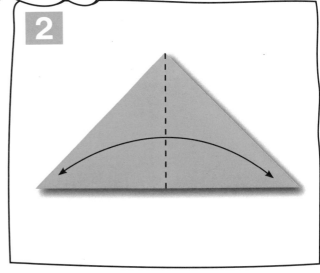

2

Fold the left point to the right point and unfold.

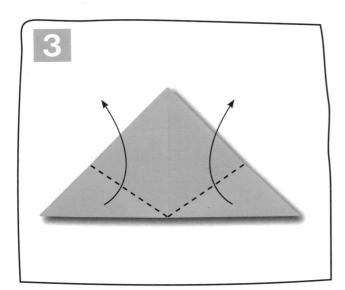

3

Fold the left and right points up.

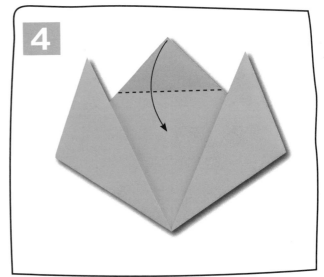

4

Fold the top point down. Turn the model over.

TIP Fold your cat out of a 3-inch (8-centimeter) paper square. Then glue it to a button magnet and stick it to your school locker or a refrigerator.

YACHTS OF FUN

An origami armada is at your fingertips! Fold a fleet of paper yachts and place them in a pond or pool. Believe it or not, they will really float!

What You Need:

square origami paper
crayons (optional)

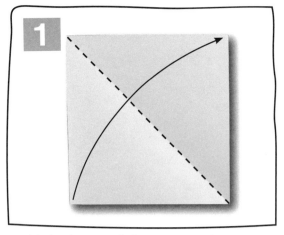

Fold the bottom-left corner to the top-right corner.

Fold the bottom point past the top edge at a slight angle. Unfold.

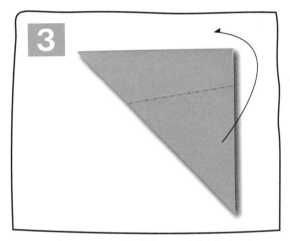

Open the paper slightly and fold the bottom point up on the creases made in step 2. The point will swing up and inside the model.

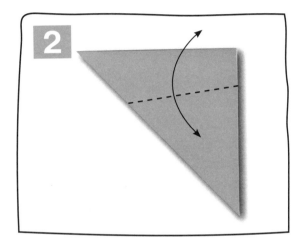

Fold the top point down and unfold.

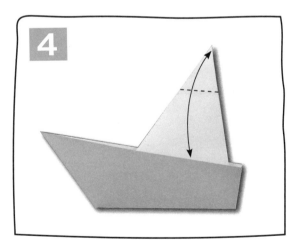

Open the model slightly and fold the top point down on the creases made in step 4. The point will swing down and inside the model.

TIP Color both sides of your yacht's bottom edges with a crayon. The crayon wax will protect the paper edges in the water. Your yacht will float longer.

WINDSURF RACER

Go windsurfing without ever getting wet!
Just take a deep breath, and puff this tiny
model all the way across the table.

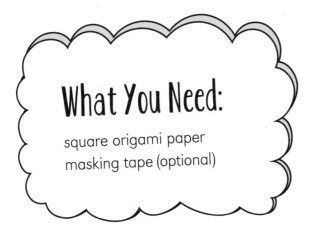

What You Need:

square origami paper
masking tape (optional)

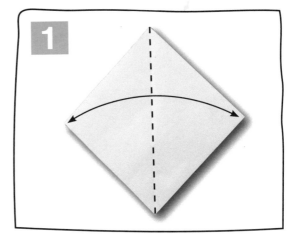

1

Fold the left point to the right point and unfold.

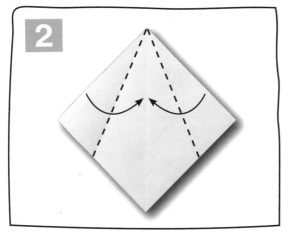

2

Fold the left and right edges to the center.

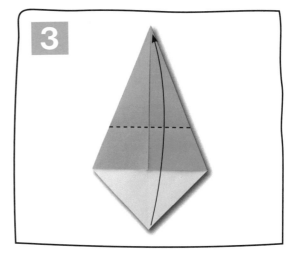

3

Fold the bottom point to the top point.

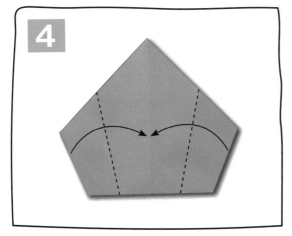

4

Fold the left and right edges to the center.

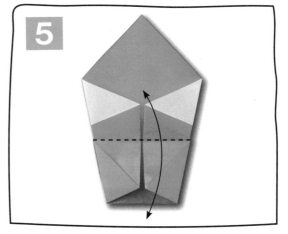

5

Fold the top layer down and unfold halfway.

TIP Use masking tape to mark a starting line and finish line on a large table. Then challenge your friends to a race. Line up several windsurfers and see who can blow their racer across the finish line first.

PENCIL POCKET

Don't lose your pencils in your backpack or locker. Keep them organized and easy to find with this handy pencil pocket.

What You Need:

square origami paper

glue and button magnets (optional)

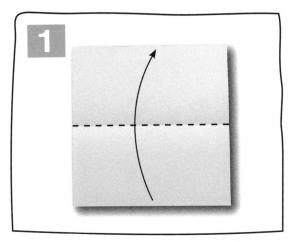

Fold the bottom edge to the top edge.

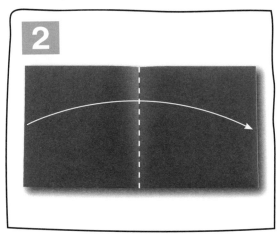

Fold the left edge to the right edge.

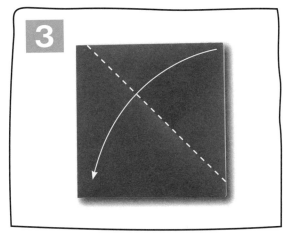

Fold the top layer's top-right corner toward the bottom-left corner so there is about a .5 inch (1.3 cm) space between them.

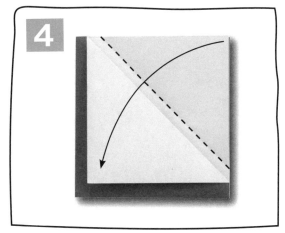

Fold the second layer's top-right corner toward the bottom-left corner so there is about a 1 inch (2.5 cm) space between them.

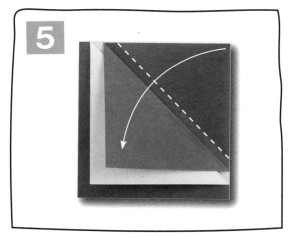

Fold the third layer's top-right corner toward the bottom-left corner so there is about a 1.5 inch (3.8 cm) space between them.

Fold the top-left and bottom-right corners behind the model. Allow them to overlap slightly in the back.

TIP Glue two button magnets to the back of your pencil pocket and stick it to any magnetic surface.

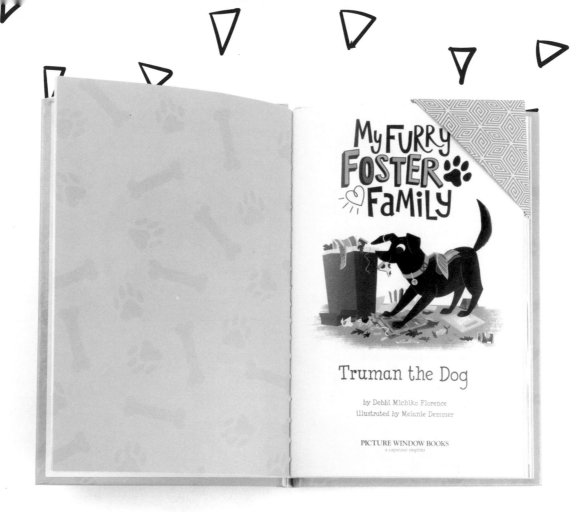

CORNER KEEPER

Never lose your spot in a book again. Simply fold this bookmark and slide it snugly onto the last page you read.

What You Need:

square origami paper
glue and craft scraps (optional)

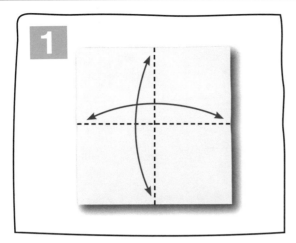

1

Fold the paper in half in both directions. Rotate.

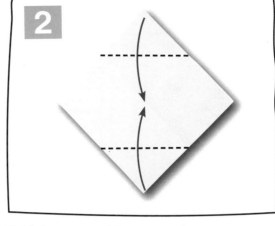

2

Fold the top and bottom points to the center crease.

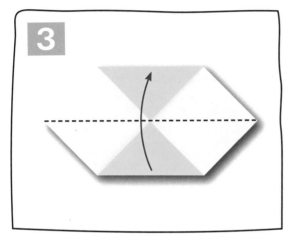

3

Fold the model in half.

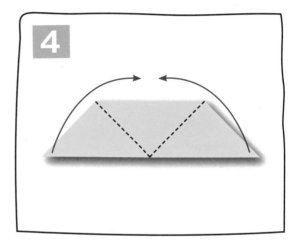

4

Fold the bottom edges to the center crease. Turn the model over.

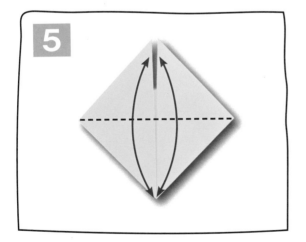

5

Fold the top points to the bottom point and unfold.

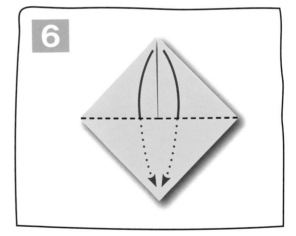

6

Tuck the top points inside the pocket.

TIP Decorate your corner keeper bookmark with craft scraps and glue to show off your artistic style!

RING WING FLING

Impress your friends with a paper airplane like no other. Just give this ring-shaped wing a fling to see it glide through the air.

What You Need:

square origami paper

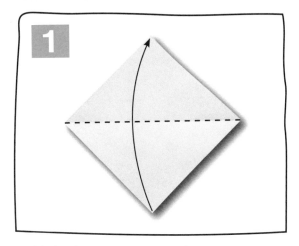

1 Fold the bottom point to the top point.

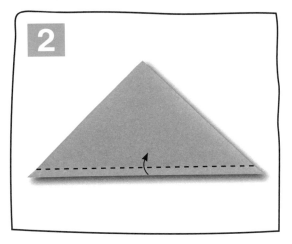

2 Fold the bottom edge up to make a narrow strip.

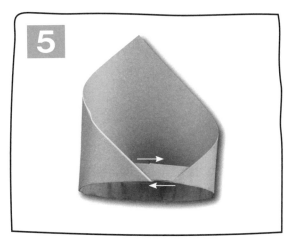

3 Fold the bottom edge up again.

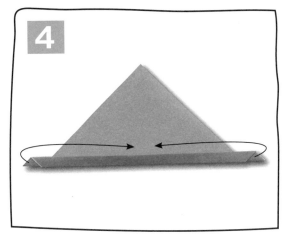

4 Bend the model to bring the ends of the strip together.

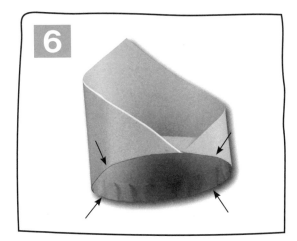

5 Tuck one end of the strip inside the other end as far as it will go.

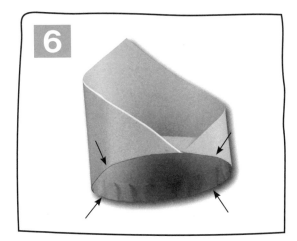

6 Shape the ring into a smooth circle with your fingers.

TIP Hold the pointed end of the ring with your index finger and thumb. Release the ring wing with a gentle forward push. Hold it high when you launch it to make it glide farther.

EXPLODING ENVELOPE

Add pizzazz to your party invitations. This envelope will burst with excitement when your friends pull its tab to open it.

What You Need:

square origami paper
scissors and wrapping paper scraps (optional)

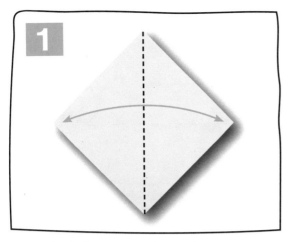

1

Fold the left point to the right point and unfold.

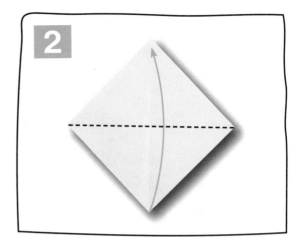

2

Fold the bottom point to the top point.

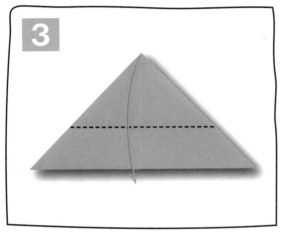

3

Fold the top layer past the bottom edge.

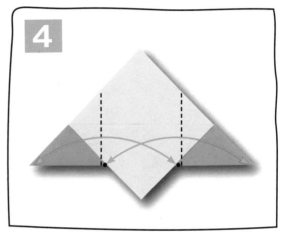

4

Fold the left and right points to the dots and unfold.

5

Tuck the left point inside the right point.

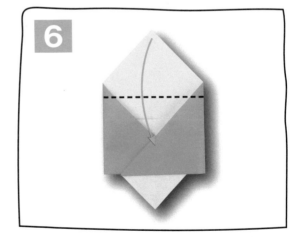

6

Fold the top point down.

TIP Cut scraps of wrapping paper into tiny pieces and add them to the envelope with your party invitation. When the envelope's tab is pulled to open it, the confetti will burst out!

TABLETOP HOOPS

Shoot some hoops without ever leaving the table. Fold this mini basketball hoop and ball. Then challenge your friends to a free throw contest.

What You Need:

printer paper
small paper scrap

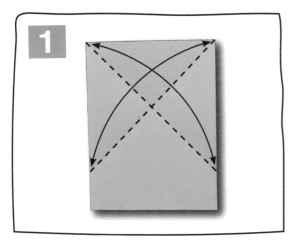

1 Fold the top corners to their opposite edges and unfold. Turn the paper over.

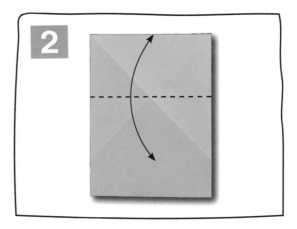

2 Fold the top edge down so its corners meet the ends of the creases made in step 1. Unfold and turn the paper over.

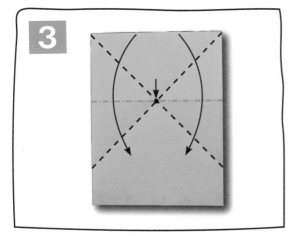

3 Push the paper at the dot and pull the top edge down. The top layer of the paper will form a triangle.

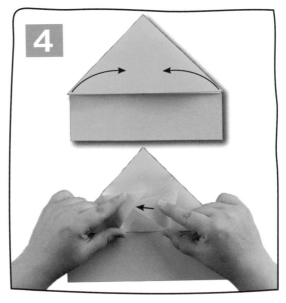

Curl the left and right points toward each other. Tuck one point inside the other.

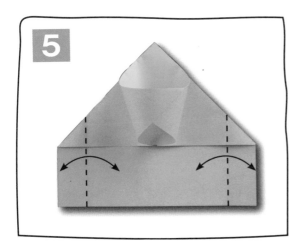

Fold the left and right edges and unfold halfway.

6 Crumple up a small scrap of paper to make a ball.

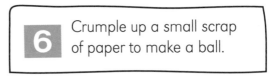

TIP Place your hoop on the end of a long table. Try shooting baskets from the other end of the table. See how many baskets you can make in a row.

MAGIC RABBIT

Origami can make you feel like a magician. Especially when you make a rabbit appear with a single square of paper!

What You Need:

square origami paper

glue, googly eyes, pom-pom, and marker (optional)

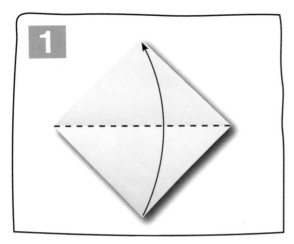

Fold the bottom point to the top point.

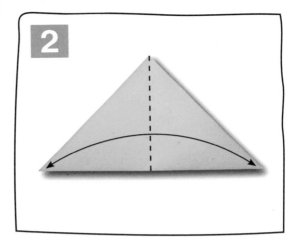

Fold the left point to the right point and unfold.

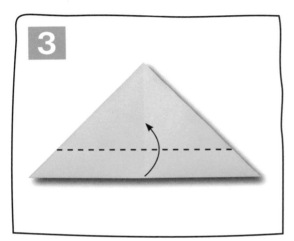

Fold the bottom edge. Make this fold about 1 inch (2.5 cm) above the edge.

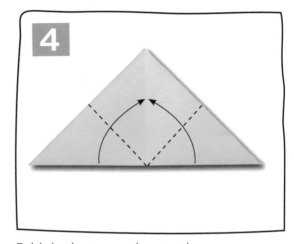

Fold the bottom edges to the center crease.

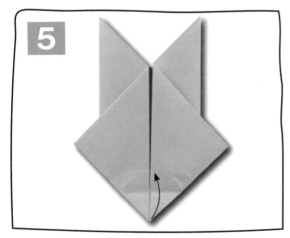

Fold the bottom point up. Turn the model over.

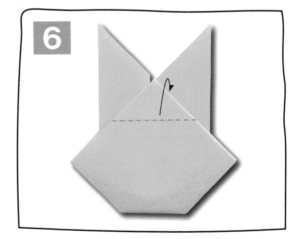

Fold the top layer's point behind to tuck it inside the model.

TIP Give your rabbit a fun face with googly eyes, a pom-pom nose, and hand-drawn whiskers.

GRACEFUL SWAN

Few birds are more graceful than a swan. This paper version highlights the swan's beauty by using both sides of the paper.

What You Need:

square origami paper

cardstock, paper scraps, markers, scissors, and glue (optional)

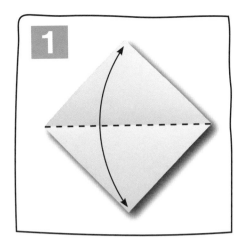

Fold the top point to the bottom point and unfold.

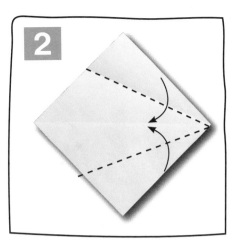

Fold the edges to the center crease. Turn the model over.

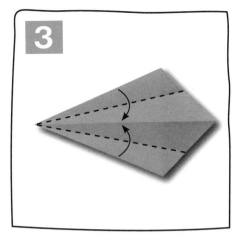

Fold the edges to the center crease.

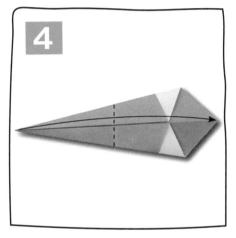

Fold the left point to the right point.

Fold the top layer's point.

Fold the top half of the model behind the bottom half.

Pull the swan's neck and head up.

TIP Fold a piece of cardstock in half to make a simple greeting card. Use paper scraps and markers to decorate the front of the card like a pond. Then glue your paper swan to the pond to complete the scene.

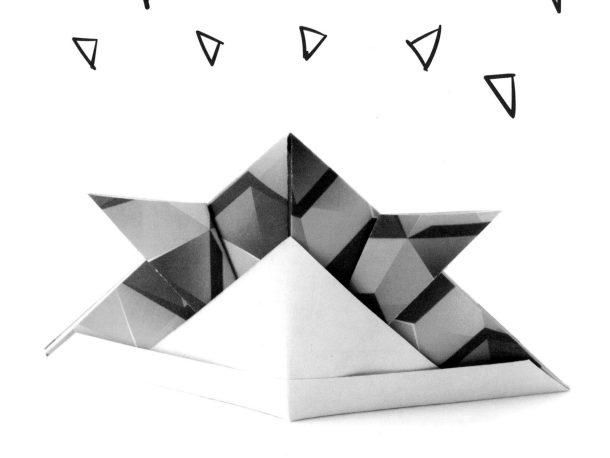

WARRIOR HELMET

Samurai warriors wore helmets called *kabuto* into battle. This paper kabuto makes the perfect pencil topper for your battle against homework!

What You Need:

square origami paper
glue, eraser cap, and pencil
(optional)

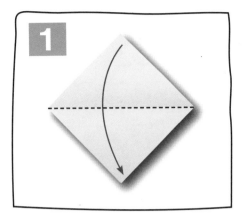

1 Fold the top point to the bottom point.

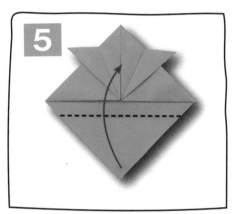

2 Fold the corners to the bottom point.

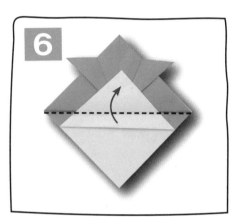

3 Fold the flaps up to the top point.

4 Fold the top layer of each flap to the side.

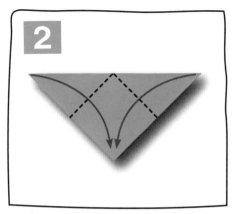

5 Fold the top layer of the bottom point up.

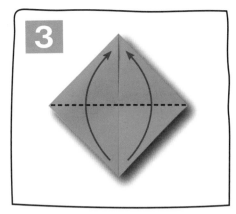

6 Fold along the bottom edge of the helmet to make a brim.

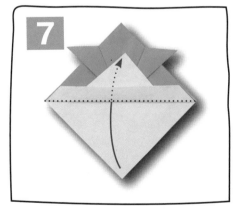

7 Fold the bottom corner into the helmet.

TIP Glue your origami samurai helmet to an eraser cap. Then slide the cap onto the end of your pencil to complete the pencil topper.

STELLAR STAR

Put spare scraps of wrapping paper and origami paper to good use. Cut them into long, thin strips, and fold them into amazing little stars!

What You Need:

.5-inch by 10-inch (1.3 cm by 25 cm) strip of paper

sewing needle and thread (optional)

1

Tie the left end of the paper strip into a knot.

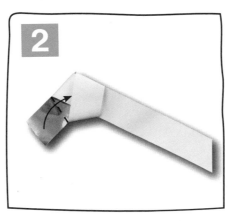

2

Tuck the short strip under the top layer.

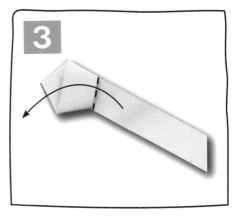

3

Fold the long strip across the knot. The strip will overlap the edge opposite your fold.

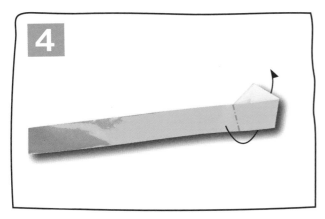

4

Fold the long strip behind the knot.

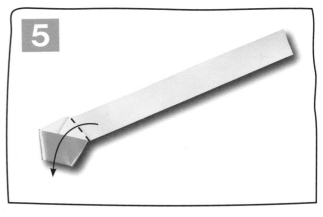

5

Continue folding the long strip across and behind the knot.

6

Tuck the remaining short strip under the top layer of the knot.

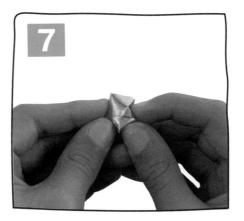

7

Use your fingernail to gently press in each side of the knot to puff up the star.

TIP Make dozens of stellar stars. Then sprinkle them on a table like confetti, or string them together with a sewing needle and thread to make garland.

POM-POM, PLEASE!

Pom-poms are simple and easy to make. Experiment with different shapes and colors. The possibilities are endless!

What You Need:

scissors
yarn
googly eyes
pipe cleaners
fork/cardboard (optional)

What You Do:

1 Cut a piece of yarn as long as your hand. Lay it between your two middle fingers.

2 Wrap more yarn loosely around the outside of your hand, about 20 times.

3 With your free hand, loosely tie the piece of yarn that's between your fingers around the wrapped yarn.

4 Slip the wrapped yarn off your hand and pull the yarn tie tight. Double knot it.

5 Cut the two yarn loops in half and trim your pom-pom.

6 To make animals, use short pieces of yarn to tie pom-poms together. Add googly eyes and pipe cleaners for feelers/horns.

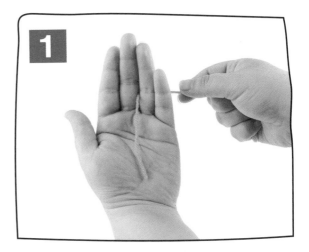

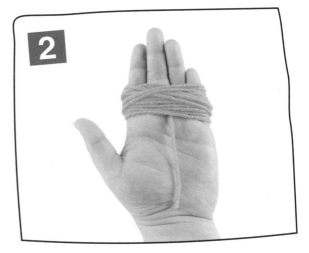

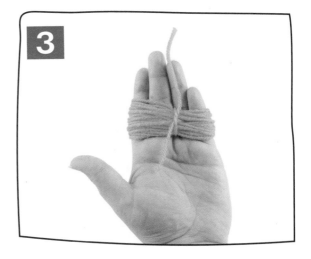

TIP To make a smaller pom-pom, use a fork instead of your hand. You can also wrap yarn around a piece of cardboard.

SMILE AND BE HAPPY DOLL

Want to make someone smile? Make this simple stick doll and give it as a gift. Clip it to a friend's backpack or put it in a locker to remind someone to smile.

What You Need:

yarn

large hole beads

scissors

quick-drying glue

stick

fabric pieces

craft magnet or
   clothespin (optional)

marker (optional)

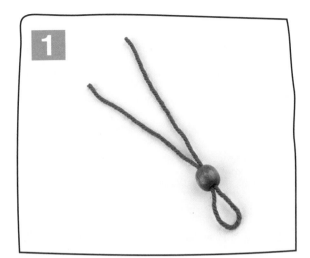

What You Do:

1 Cut a piece of yarn as long as
your hand. Fold it in half and
thread the loop through the hole
of a bead.

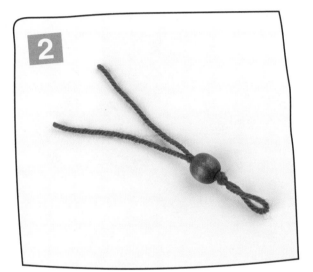

2 Tie the loop of yarn in a knot,
tight up against the bead. The
loop should be long enough to
look like hair. Cut the loop in half
and pull apart the strands to
create "hair".

3 Glue the end of the bead without
the knot to the top of a small
stick. Wrap the two yarn strands
around the top end of the stick to
look like a neck.

4 Glue fabric pieces to the stick to
look like clothes. Add yarn pieces
for extra decoration.

TIP Glue a craft magnet or clothespin to the back
of the doll. Add faces with a marker, if you wish.

YARN ANIMAL

Go wild! Use your imagination and shape foil into any animal you can think of. How about a hummingbird? Perhaps you like octopuses? Pick one and get making!

What You Need:

foil
yarn
scissors
cardboard
toothpicks
quick-drying glue (optional)

What You Do:

1 Shape foil into an animal shape.

2 Wrap the foil in yarn.

3 Use cardboard and toothpicks to add details like wings and beaks.

TIP Don't have foil? Use cardboard, or glue wooden blocks together, instead.

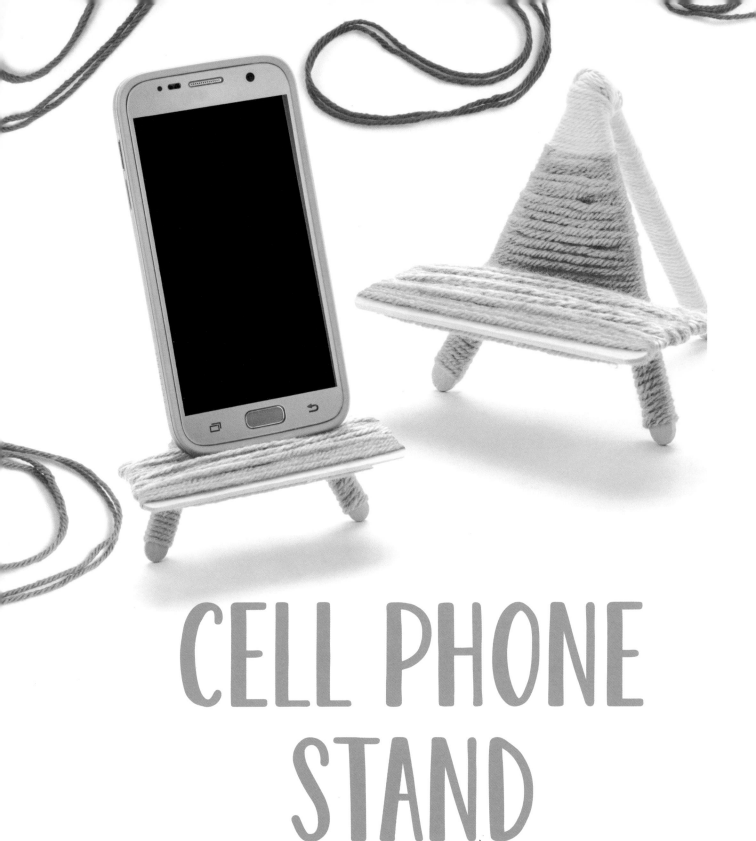

CELL PHONE STAND

Know someone who could use a cell phone stand? Check out this simple project you can make in minutes. Leave it on someone's desk as a fun surprise!

What You Need:

7–8 craft sticks
tape/quick-drying glue
yarn
cardboard (optional)

What You Do:

1 Lay two craft sticks together in an upside down V-shape. Tape or glue the sticks together where they meet.

2 Glue a third stick to the point of the V, so the V stands up.

3 Glue three or four other craft sticks together at the edges to create a flat surface. Then glue one edge to the center of the upside down V, to form a shelf.

4 Wrap the stand in yarn.

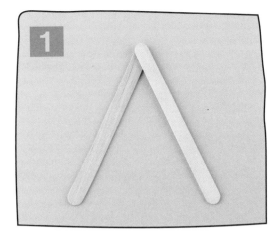

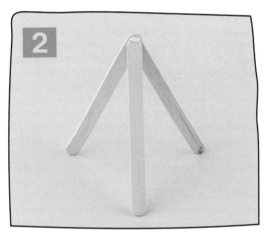

TIP Cut any shape you'd like out of cardboard, the same size as a phone. Glue one craft stick to the back so it stands up. Wrap the shape in yarn. Set a phone against this holder for another option.

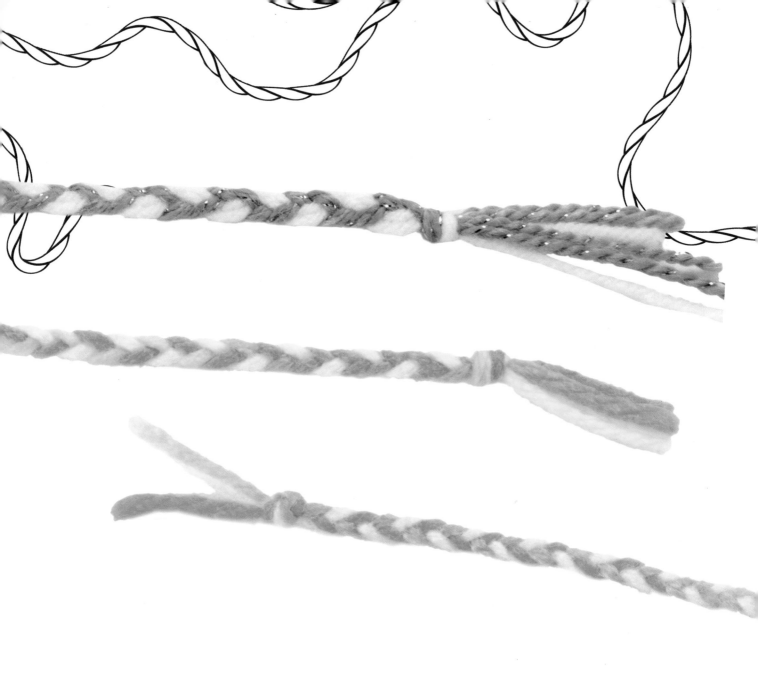

BRAIDING

Whether you already know how to braid, or you just want to learn, these friendship bracelets will have you braiding in a snap. Get your friends braiding too, and then exchange bracelets!

What You Need:

3 pieces of yarn,
about 12 inches
(30 centimeters) long

tape

What You Do:

1 Tie the three pieces of yarn together at one end. Tape the knot to a table or other surface.

2 Cross the right string over the middle string. Then cross the left string over the middle string.

3 Repeat until you get to the end of the yarn. Tie the ends of yarn together to finish the braid.

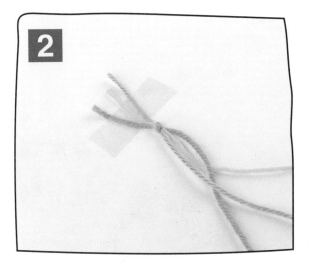

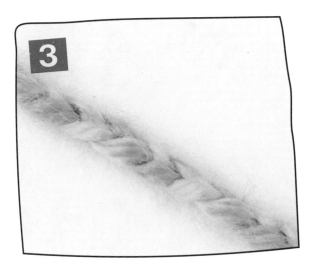

TIP Turn any braid into a friendship bracelet. Simply tie each of the ends together around a friend's wrist.

DRAGON EGG SURPRISE

What can hold an amazing surprise?
A dragon's egg, of course! Your friends
will love this fun-filled egg.

What You Need:

3 pieces of yarn, 48 inches
   (1.2 meters) long
tape
plastic egg
quick-drying glue
toys/candy for inside the egg

What You Do:

1 Braid the three strands of yarn together. Tie the ends in a knot.

2 Wrap the braid around one half of a plastic egg that opens. Use quick-drying glue to hold the braid in place.

3 Repeat steps 2–3 for the other half of the egg.

4 Hide surprises inside the egg.

FEATHER BOOKMARK

Save your spot with these fancy yarn feathers!
Your favorite book will thank you!

What You Need:

yarn

scissors

beads (optional)

What You Do:

1 Cut one piece of yarn as long as your arm. Fold it in half, with the loop facing upward. This will be the middle of the feather.

2 Cut two more pieces of yarn as long as your hand. Fold both pieces in half. Slide one of these loops under the first loop you made so its tails are pointing to the right.

3 Slide the third loop under the second loop and over the first loop. Its tails should point to the left. Pull the left and right tails of yarn tight.

4 Repeat steps 2–3 with more pieces of yarn to make the feather.

5 Trim the edges to create a feather shape.

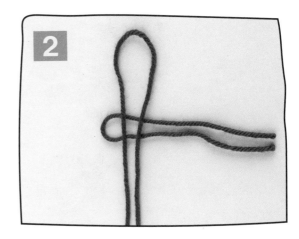

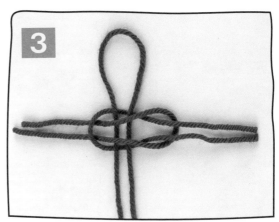

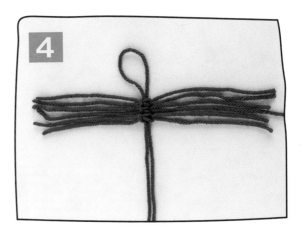

TIP You can make this a zipper pull instead of a bookmark. Add beads to the feathers. Then attach the feather to a zipper with more yarn.

103

HUG IT

Don't throw away those plastic drinking straws!
Recycle them and weave a handy hugger for your
water bottle or a mug of hot chocolate!

What You Need:

- 3 pieces of yarn, about 15 inches (38 cm) long
- 3 plastic straws
- tape
- 1 piece of yarn, about 30 inches (76 cm) long
- button (optional)

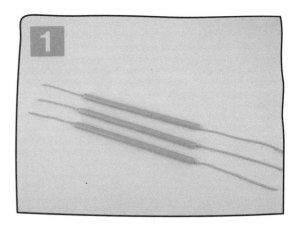

What You Do:

1 Thread each of the smaller pieces of yarn through a straw.

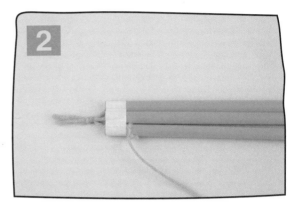

2 Tie the yarn in a knot at one end. Tape the straws together below the knot. Tie the end of the long piece of yarn to one of the outside straws.

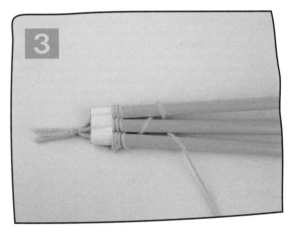

3 Weave the long piece of yarn in and out of the straws. Stop weaving when you get to the other end of the straws.

4 Remove the tape. Hold the top of the weaving and pull each straw out, one at a time.

5 Tie the tails of the yarn together around a bottle or mug.

TIP Add more straws to make a wider piece. To add a second color, simply tie on a different color of yarn and continue the weave. Glue a button on for an extra touch!

MUSTACHE ME

Ever wanted a fun mustache? You can make your own! You'll laugh out loud at this super simple, super silly mustache.

What You Need:

1 piece of yarn, about 20 inches (51 cm) long

pipe cleaner

additional yarn

scissors

What You Do:

1 Tie the yarn together to make a loop. To test it, put one end around each ear. If it is too short, add more yarn to the loop. If it's too long, tie a knot and make a loop to fit.

2 Set the loop on top of the pipe cleaner.

3 Cut a piece of yarn 10 inches (25 cm) long and fold it in half. Slide the loop under the pipe cleaner.

4 Pull the tails of that piece through the loop. Tug it tight.

5 Cut more pieces of yarn and tie on the same way all they way down the pipe cleaner. Fold over the ends of the pipe cleaner so the wires aren't showing.

6 Bend into a mustache shape and trim the yarn to make different looks. Hook the yarn loops around your ears.

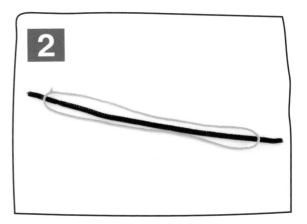

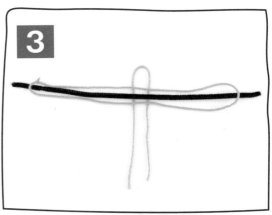

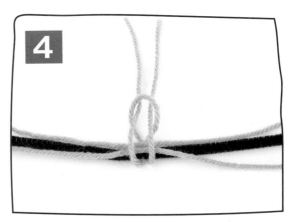

STICK TO IT

Decorate your locker or room with this colorful wall hanging. Pick your favorite colors to brighten up a simple stick. Yarn can turn anything into a work of art!

What You Do:

1 Cut enough pieces of yarn to cover the length of the stick. Fold each piece in half and line them up next to each other.

2 Place the stick across the middle of all the yarn pieces.

3 Bring the tail ends of one piece of yarn through its loop and pull tight. Repeat for the remaining pieces of yarn.

4 Once you've tied all pieces of yarn, trim the ends at an angle or all the same length.

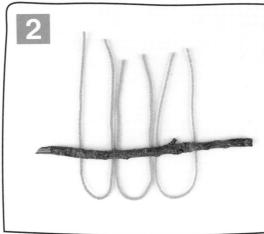

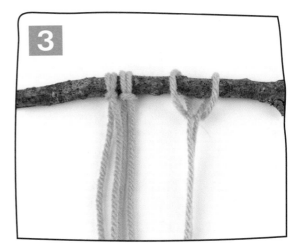

YARN FLOWERPOT

Turn a plain plastic bottle into a flowerpot. Fill it with real plants or make your own. You can even use yarn to make a holder for your new pot.

What You Need:

plastic water bottle
1 piece of yarn, about 25 feet
  (8 m) long
additional yarn, different
  color
duct tape/hot glue
key ring (optional)

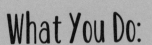

What You Do:

1 Ask an adult to cut off the spout of the plastic water bottle.

2 Loop the yarn through the spout. Tape or glue one end of the yarn to the inside of the spout.

3 Wrap yarn through and around the spout. To change colors, tie on another piece of yarn and hide the knot inside the spout.

4 Add fake plants to the yarn pot.

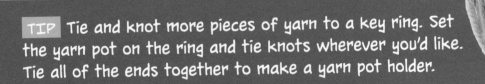

TIP Tie and knot more pieces of yarn to a key ring. Set the yarn pot on the ring and tie knots wherever you'd like. Tie all of the ends together to make a yarn pot holder.

CATAPULT

Try launching yarn pom-poms, marshmallows, or even paper balls with this quick and easy catapult. Bombs away!

What You Need:

8 craft sticks

yarn

quick-drying glue

small paper cupcake liner or
  bottle cap

scissors

plastic lid

small plastic cup

yarn pom-pom

What You Do:

1 Stack six craft sticks together.
Wrap them in yarn on both ends.

2 Stack two craft sticks. Wrap them
in yarn on one end.

3 Slide the open end of the two-
stick stack over the larger stack.

4 Glue a paper liner to the open
end of the stack of two sticks.

5 Press down on the stick by the
paper liner and let it spring back
up. You're ready to launch!

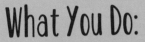

TIP Slide the sticks up or down on
the larger stack of sticks to change
the projection of your pom-pom.

MOVING TARGET

Make a moving target for your
catapult. Cut a hole in the middle of
the lid, large enough for a small cup
to fit inside. Wrap yarn around the
lid and set the target in front of the
catapult. Can you get the pom-pom
into the cup?

STICK WEAVING

You can use almost anything to make your own loom. Start this project yourself and then make it into a larger piece of artwork for your classroom. Now, that's teamwork!

What You Need:

glue
craft sticks
yarn

What You Do:

1 Glue two craft sticks together to make an X.

2 Start in the middle of the X. Wrap different colors of yarn around the sticks, weaving in and out of the X.

3 To change yarn colors, tie on another piece of yarn.

4 End the weave and tie the yarn tail onto another woven piece in the back.

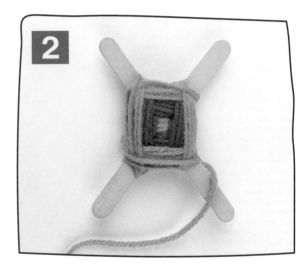

TIP Ask your friends to make a bunch of different stick shapes. Glue or tie the woven shapes together with yarn to make abstract art.

EARBUD BRACELET

Don't toss broken earbud cords. Use them to whip up this cool and colorful bracelet.

What You Need:

2 broken earbud cords
scissors
ruler
tape
small beads

What You Do:

1 Peel apart and cut the cords into three pieces, each 30 inches (76 centimeters) long.

2 Line up the cords and fold them in half.

3 Pull out the folded end of one cord to make a small loop. Tie the other cords around the loop.

4 Tape the loop to a table. Then braid the cords by overlapping them one after another. Every four to six braids, thread small beads onto one of the cords.

5 Keep braiding until the bracelet fits around your wrist. Tie the end of the cords into a knot. Trim down the loose ends.

6 Remove the tape. Thread the knot through the loop to finish the bracelet.

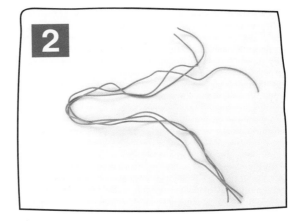

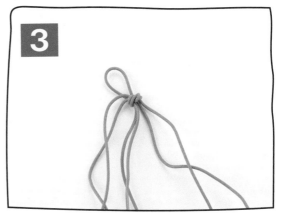

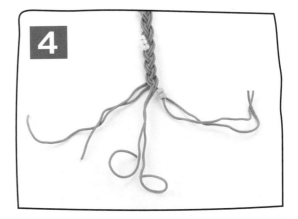

TIP Braid colorful string or yarn into your bracelet to add extra pops of color.

WEARABLE WASHERS

Metal washers are not just for the workshop. Glam them up with permanent markers to make this nifty necklace.

What You Need:

4–8 metal washers, different sizes
permanent markers
3–7 small paper clips
24-inch- (61-cm-) long cord
scissors

What You Do:

1 Decorate one side of each washer with permanent markers. Blow on them to dry.

2 Arrange the washers in a fun pattern.

3 Connect the washers with small paper clips.

4 Tie one end of the cord to one side of your washer arrangement.

5 Thread the loose end of the cord through a washer on the other side of the washer arrangement. Pinch the cord tight and put the necklace on.

6 Adjust the loose cord until you like the length of the necklace. Then tie it in place and cut off any extra cord.

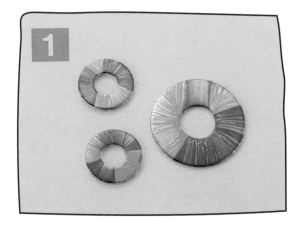

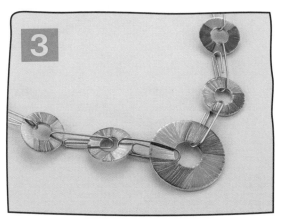

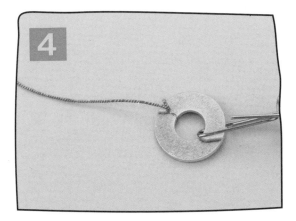

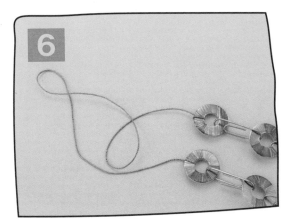

KITTY LANTERN

Rescue a milk jug from your recycling bin.
Then upcycle it into this cute kitty to light
up your yard or room.

What You Need:

large milk jug
utility knife
markers
felt
scissors
hot glue gun
2 pipe cleaners
colored tissue paper
battery-powered tea light

What You Do:

1 Ask an adult to cut off the milk jug's spout and handle with the utility knife.

2 Draw a kitty nose, eyes, and mouth on one side of the jug.

3 Cut the felt into shapes that look like cat ears. Glue them above the kitty's face.

4 Fold each pipe cleaner in half. Then glue them on either side of the nose to make whiskers.

5 Fill the inside of the jug with tissue paper.

6 Turn on the tea light and nest it inside the tissue paper.

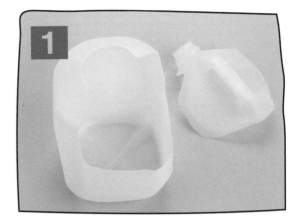

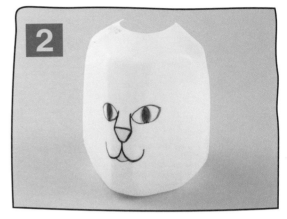

TIP What other kinds of animals can you make? Try making a puppy, turkey, or bear.

FIREFLY FRIEND

Brighten your day every time you open your locker with a firefly friend. It's charming and easy to make.

What You Need:

plastic water bottle
scissors
hot glue gun
metal bottle cap
2 googly eyes
LED bulb
CR2032 button battery
electrical tape
button magnet

What You Do:

1 Cut a small pair of wings out of the water bottle. Hot glue them to the top of the bottle cap.

2 Glue the googly eyes to the bottle cap right below the wings.

3 Slide the LED onto the button battery. The short wire should touch the negative (-) side. The long wire should touch the positive (+) side. Wrap a short piece of electrical tape around the battery to keep the LED in place.

4 Glue the battery inside the bottle cap so the LED stands up behind the wings.

5 Place the bottle cap on the magnet.

6 Stick the firefly on your locker for a fun glowing friend.

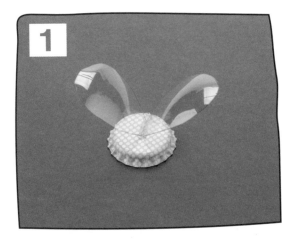

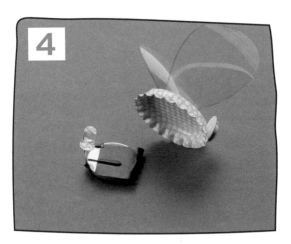

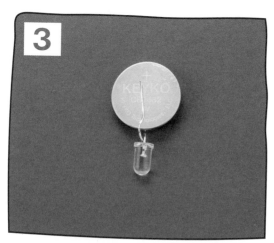

TIP To turn off the firefly, remove the magnet and slide one of the LED leads out from under the tape.

CRAYON CREATION

What can you do with short and broken crayons? Break them up even more to make a colorful design of the first letter in your name!

What You Need:

cardboard (any size)
pencil
old crayons
scissors
hot glue gun

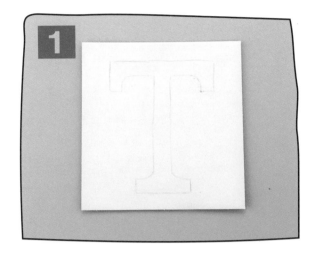

What You Do:

1 Lightly sketch a large letter on the cardboard.

2 Pick out a variety of crayons and peel off their paper wrappers.

3 Break the crayons into pieces that will cover the letter's shape. To make small pieces, cut through the crayons with scissors.

4 Lay out the crayons on top of the letter.

5 Once arranged, remove the crayon pieces one at a time. Carefully hot glue each piece in place.

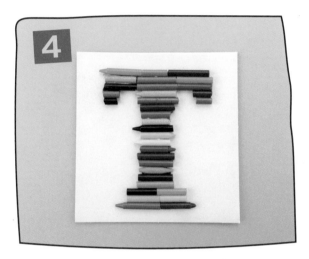

TIP Try making other colorful designs with crayons, such as flowers or hearts.

BFF PUZZLE NECKLACES

A puzzle isn't much fun when a piece goes missing. But don't despair. Just turn the remaining pieces into one-of-a-kind friendship necklaces!

What You Need:

3 connecting puzzle pieces
markers
hole punch
3 24-inch- (61-cm-) long cords

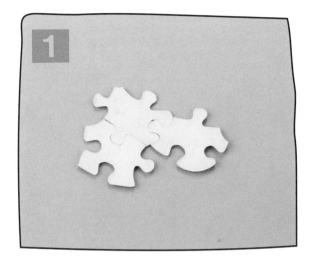

What You Do:

1 Connect the puzzle pieces and flip them over.

2 Use the markers to create a design or message across the back of all the pieces.

3 Punch a hole in the top of each puzzle piece.

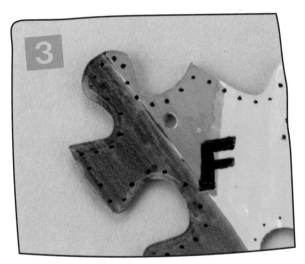

4 Separate the puzzle pieces and thread a cord onto each one. Tie the ends of each cord to make necklaces.

5 Give the necklaces to your best friends!

TIP Boost team spirit! Make enough connecting necklaces for the teammates of a sport you play.

TIN MAN WIND CHIME

Don't leave tin cans clanging around in your recycling bin. Use a couple to whip up this little tin man wind chime.

What You Need:

tall tin can
short tin can
hammer
nail
24-inch (61-cm)
   piece of yarn
4 5-inch (13-cm)
   pieces of yarn

9 metal washers
ruler
toothpick
hot glue gun
2 googly eyes
marker

What You Do:

1 Ask an adult to punch a hole in the top of each can with the hammer and nail.

2 Fold the 24-inch (61-cm) piece of yarn in half and tie its loose ends to a washer. About 2 inches (5 cm) up from the washer, tie a triple knot in the long loop of yarn.

3 Thread the yarn above the knot through the tall can, and then up through the short can. Use a toothpick to help push the yarn through the holes.

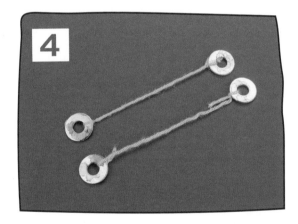

4 Tie washers onto the ends of the remaining pieces of yarn.

5 Hot glue one washer from each piece of yarn to the bottom can to make arms and legs.

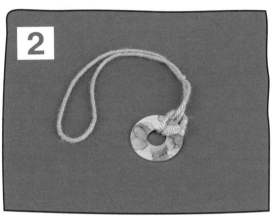

6 Hot glue the googly eyes and draw a mouth on the top can to complete your tin man wind chime.

T-SHIRT PILLOW

Do you have a favorite T-shirt that doesn't fit anymore? Don't toss it! Turn it into a no-sew pillow to jazz up your room.

What You Need:

T-shirt
scissors
ruler
fiberfill stuffing

What You Do:

1 Lay the T-shirt on a flat surface. Cut off the arms, bottom hem, and neck of the shirt to create two identical rectangles.

2 Keeping the rectangles stacked flat, cut 3-inch (8-cm) squares out of each corner.

3 Beginning near one corner, cut 3-inch- (8-cm-) deep slits evenly on all four edges of both layers. Space each slit about 1 inch (2.5 cm) apart.

4 Keeping the fabric stacked, tie each tab, one after another, into a double knot.

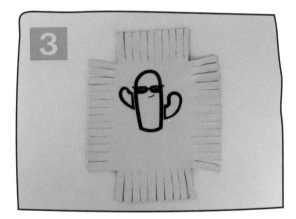

5 When only six tabs remain, stuff fiberfill though the opening to fill the pillow.

6 Once stuffed, finish tying the remaining tabs.

TIP Sweatshirt fabric or old fleece blankets work well for this project too!

POURED PAINT LUMINARY

It's easy to add a splash of color to an old jar. With some glitter and lights, this luminary will really make your room glow.

What You Need:

craft stick
1 tablespoon (15 mL) decoupage
    glue
1 teaspoon (5 mL) water
food coloring
disposable cup
glass jar
glitter
battery-powered fairy lights

What You Do:

1   Use a craft stick to mix together
    the decoupage glue, water, and
    15 drops of food coloring in a
    disposable cup.

2   Pour the mixture into the glass jar.
    Add a few sprinkles of glitter.

3   Swirl the mixture around in the jar
    to coat the inside.

4   Pour any excess mixture back into
    the disposable cup and throw
    away.

5   Wait a couple minutes as the
    decoupage glue dries very quickly.
    Once dry, add the fairy lights to
    the jar.

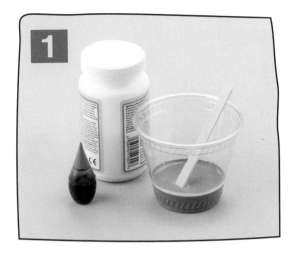

PINWHEEL COLLAGE

Don't throw out your old magazines.
Turn their glossy pages into colorful art!

What You Need:

magazine
scissors
ruler
hot glue gun
6-inch- (15-cm-) long string

What You Do:

1 Cut a page from the magazine. Accordion fold it along one of its long edges by making creases every 0.5 inch (1 cm).

2 Fold the creased page in half. Glue the edges that meet together to make a fan.

3 Repeat steps 1 and 2 to make two more fans.

4 Glue the edges of the three fans together to make a pinwheel.

5 Repeat steps 1 through 4 to make several more pinwheels. Make smaller pinwheels by accordion folding the short edges of the magazine pages.

6 Glue the pinwheels together to make a colorful collage. Then loop a string and glue it to the top of the collage so it can hang.

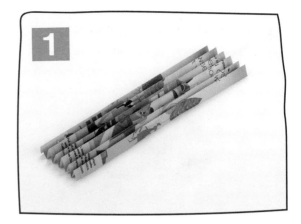

TIP Try different types of paper for this project. Book pages and wrapping paper work well too.

CELL PHONE SLEEVE

Check your closets for a long-forgotten necktie. Then upcycle the colorful castoff into a stylish cell phone case.

What You Need:

old necktie
ruler
scissors
hot glue gun
self-adhesive hook and
    loop fasteners

What You Do:

1 Cut off the wide end of the necktie 14 inches (36 cm) from its tip. Set the rest of the tie aside.

2 Open the flaps on the back of the tie. Fold the top edge down 0.5 inch (1 cm) and glue in place.

3 Place your phone in the center of the tie. Fold the bottom edge up and top edge down to create a pocket. Remove the phone and glue the center seam in place.

4 Tuck the cut edge of the tie inside the pocket and glue the opening closed.

5 Stick the fasteners to the inside of the tip and the face of the case to make a closable flap.

6 Cut the narrow end of the tie 9 inches (23 cm) from its tip. Glue the ends together to make a loop.

7 Glue the end of the loop about 1 inch (2.5 cm) below the back of the case's top edge.

TIP Slide your cell phone into the case and hang it in your locker.

137

SNOWFLAKE ORNAMENT

Raid the recycling bin for cardboard tubes. Then make them into a bunch of beautiful snowflakes.

What You Need:

cardboard tube
ruler
pencil
scissors
hot glue gun
glue stick
glitter
6-inch- (15-cm-) long string

What You Do:

1 Flatten the cardboard tube. Mark lines every 0.25 inch (0.6 cm) along the flattened edge with a pencil.

2 Cut along the lines from step 1 to make oval slices.

3 Arrange four slices in a star pattern. Hot glue the points at the center to form a basic snowflake shape.

4 Fold four more slices in half. Fit each folded slice between a main section of the snowflake shape. Hot glue them at the center.

5 Rub glue stick onto the face of the snowflake. Dip the face of the snowflake into a pile of glitter.

6 Tie a string in a loop around one point of the snowflake to hang.

TIP Just like real snowflakes, the designs you can create are unlimited. Layer the ovals or slice them in half to make different designs.

PERFECT PAINTED PLANTER

What can you do with a used water bottle? Pamper your plants with the perfect painted planter!

What You Need:

plastic bottle
utility knife
acrylic paint
paintbrush
hole punch
12-inch- (30-cm-) long string
soil and plant

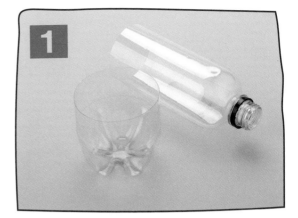

What You Do:

1 Ask an adult to cut off the bottom third of the plastic bottle with a utility knife. Recycle the top of the bottle.

2 Ask an adult to poke several holes in the bottom of the bottle with the utility knife for drainage.

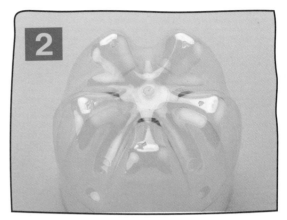

3 Decorate the bottom of the bottle with fun designs using acrylic paint. Blow on the paint to help it dry quickly.

4 Punch holes on opposite sides of the planter. Tie the string to the holes so the planter can hang.

5 Fill the bottom of the bottle with soil and plant your favorite plant in it.

TIP Hang this planter outdoors so water can freely drain from the holes in the bottom.

Looking for more projects?
YOU'RE IN LUCK!

...AMAZING... MAGIC ...TRICKS!...

BY NORM BARNHART

MORE THAN **80** MAGIC VIDEOS!

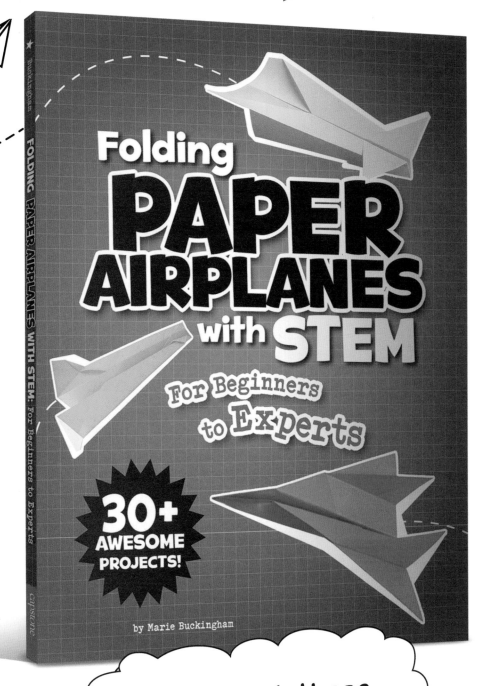

Folding PAPER AIRPLANES with STEM

For Beginners to Experts

30+ AWESOME PROJECTS!

by Marie Buckingham

Check out these other fun Capstone books, and you'll be busy for days!

Dabble Lab is published by Capstone Press, a Capstone imprint.
1710 Roe Crest Drive, North Mankato, Minnesota 56003
capstonepub.com

Library of Congress Cataloging-in-Publication Data
Names: Harbo, Christopher L., author. | Schuette, Sarah L., 1976- author. | Enz, Tammy, author. | Makuc, Lucy, illustrator.
Title: 10-minute fun and easy projects : 65 craft activities you can make in a flash / by Christopher Harbo, Sarah L. Schuette, and Tammy Enz ; illustrated by Lucy Makuc.
Other titles: Ten-minute fun and easy projects
Description: North Mankato, Minnesota : Capstone Press, a Capstone imprint, [2021] | Series: 10-minute makers | Audience: Ages 8–11 | Audience: Grades 2–3 | Summary: "Got 10 minutes? Get making with a jam-packed collection of quick, self-guided projects and activities that won't break the bank. From origami, drawing, and yarn creations to games, gadgets, and upcycled crafts, these fun projects will get kids making in 10 minutes or less"—Provided by publisher.
Identifiers: LCCN 2021006185 (print) | LCCN 2021006186 (ebook) | ISBN 9781663934147 (paperback) | ISBN 9781663934154 (pdf)
Subjects: LCSH: Handicraft for children—Juvenile literature.
Classification: LCC TT160 .H3564 2021 (print) | LCC TT160 (ebook) | DDC 745.5083—dc23
LC record available at https://lccn.loc.gov/2021006185
LC ebook record available at https://lccn.loc.gov/2021006186

Editorial Credits
Designer: Tracy McCabe; Media Researcher: Jo Miller; Production Specialist: Katy LaVigne; Project Production: Marcy Morin

Photo Credits
All photographs by Capstone Studio: Karon Dubke; except TJ Thoraldson Digital Photography, 75, 79, 87; Illustrations by Lucy Makuc, 12–37

Design Elements
Shutterstock: Andriy Lipkan, Aygun Ali, balabolka, best_vector, BewWanchai, Bjoern Wylezich, casejustin, CNuisin, Devita ayu silvianingtyas, Dr Project, Epine, Evgeniya Pautova, Fafarumba, Golden Shrimp, H Art, HNK, hudhud94, Jaws_73, Jenov Jenovallen, KannaA, keport, Koritsia, Maria_Konstantinova, MG Drachal, mijatmijatovic, Milya, newelle, nichy, Olha Yerofieieva, olllikeballoon, Pacharawi Imsuwan, Ptaha I, Receh Lancar Jaya, sergio34, StockSmartStart, strizh, Tanya Sun, Tukang Desain, vectopicta, Vector-M, Vikoshkina, Vintage Love Story, Yes - Royalty Free, Zebra Finch

Printed and bound in the USA. 004270